DIGITAL PHOTOGRAPHY MASTERY

9 Tips to Master Technical Aspects Including ISO, Exposure, Metering & Shutter Speed

James Carren

For more books by this author, please visit
www.photographybooks.us

Table of Contents

Introduction

As we discussed in my book "Photography Exposure," exposure is probably the most important technical element in all of photography. I say this because an exposure is what a photograph physically *is*. Of course, you also need to pay attention to things like your composition, your intent, and your post work. But without a good exposure, all of that is a moot point. If you can't see what a photograph is of, or if the exposure is so bad that it distracts from what otherwise would be a competent and poignant photograph, then you have failed. Being technically competent is only half of the process, but I find that it is extremely important to master before you can tackle the big issues in your photography.

In the digital age, too many people mistakenly categorize themselves as photographers simply because they have a DSLR and can shoot it on auto. While this can certainly be a gateway into the world of photography, as it was for me, this does not make you a photographer. So how do you begin to become a photographer? Well, you must master your camera, and understand its functions so that you're in complete control of the outcome. That's what this book is all about.

I'm going to cover some more advanced aspects of exposure, including some of the science and math behind it, as well as the techniques of metering and bracketing. I'll explain how exposure can differ when working with different types of film, as opposed to digital. Then we'll talk about shooting modes, which can help you to become a better photographer, and work your way up to completely manual shooting. Different lighting conditions are obviously key as well, since you'll need to know how to control your exposure indoors, outdoors, and on many kinds of days. Finally, I'll talk about the editing process, and my favorite editing program, which is Camera RAW. Since we will be talking about exposure for film, we should also talk about editing that exposure. Even if you aren't a film photographer, (as I assume most of you are not), I still think learning about the original thing is beneficial. I want this to be as well rounded as it can be for its length.

Tip 1: Capture As Much As Possible in Camera

No matter what, whether you are an experienced photographer or brand new to this, I feel like capturing as much as you can in-camera is good practice. So what exactly do I mean when I say that you should capture everything in-camera? It basically means, don't rely so much on editing. Too many times, I hear clients (and even other photographers), say something along the lines of, "I like this photo, but the highlights are all blown out. I'll just fix it in post." Or, "I don't like the position of her body, can you fix it in post?"

Now, the first statement, while it does make me roll my eyes, is at least slightly reasonable. Yes, if you have a photo you really like that is *slightly* technically unsound, by all means, fix it. But if you know that you messed up that photo and you have the opportunity to shoot it again more correctly, do so. Don't just look at it and settle, and think that you can fix it later. Because while you may feel that you are saving yourself some time right now, in the long run you've just made that much more work for yourself. Fixing a problem is always so much more difficult and time consuming than you anticipate, especially when you could have just prevented it.

Don't use post work as an excuse for bad photos. If it's not shot correctly, do it again.

What about that second statement? "I don't like the position of her body, can you fix it in post?" While it is possible to put someone else's head on a different body in Photoshop and make minor adjustments to body position by layering two or three different pictures, it's not possible to change everything. For example, if you have a photo of someone who is stationary when what you really

3

wanted was for them to be jumping, you can try to splice their torso onto different legs, but more often than not, the result just looks disjointed and a little bit like Frankenstein's monster. I've had clients ask for this very thing before, and no one is ever very satisfied with the result.

Anything that's technical, anything that you do have control over, you should try to take care of while the camera is still in your hand. Be conscious and in control of the choices you make as a photographer, and save the post work for things you can't change, like a blemish here or there, or a shadow that needs a little pop of light. This book is all about familiarizing yourself with your camera so that you don't feel the need to compensate for poor technical skills. If your technical skills are strong, you then have a good basis to begin to explore what you really want to in photography. You'll be proud and save yourself a lot of unnecessary work when your images only need minor touchups.

A lot of people love to use Photoshop in order to combine multiple photos and create what's called a composite. This is different from using Photoshop to compensate for poor skills. Most of the time, when making a composite, you have to know exactly what it is you need ahead of time. For example, if you know that a scene you need to shoot is going to be backlit, which often makes the foreground over bright and the background way too dark, then you know that you'll need to take two separate photos. This will ensure that you get a proper exposure for both areas, and once composited, you can have one good composition. That is an example of a reason to use Photoshop for more than just basic edits.

Compositing can also be great for surrealism or otherworldly images. Combine to your heart's content, but remember that those photos you combine should be solid to begin with, or you'll have to spend a lot of extra time fixing them before you can combine them.

The point here is, that capturing things in-camera is a conservation of energy. It gives you time to make more work, and better work. It also cuts down on the amount of time spent in front of the computer, whether you do full fashion retouching, or compositing, or not.

Tip 2: Mastering ISO

I feel like a lot of people typically forget that there are actually three parts to exposure. Of course there is aperture and shutter speed, but there is also ISO. ISO, which is also referred to as ASA in some circles, controls the sensitivity of your camera to light. With film, you control ISO by selecting the ISO of the film you want to use beforehand, and then adjusting your camera as such, and with digital, it is controlled by a knob typically found on the top of your camera.

There are slow film speeds and fast film speeds, slow being denoted by smaller numbers, such as 100 and 200. 400 is generally accepted as a good starting point, since its speed is right in the middle of the spectrum. Film generally only goes up to about 1600, but recent digital cameras go up much higher. In darker situations, faster film speeds allow in more light, however, the higher the ISO, the more grain you'll have present in your image.

In traditional film, grain is the leftover particles of silver that remain after the development process. They create a dot-like pattern over the image. The more "dots" you have, the closer they are together, which creates a high resolution, low grain, smooth image. This is what you want. Now, when you have a lot of grain in the image (as in you can see the individual dots across the image), your image is much lower resolution. While this look can be used for aesthetic purposes to make an image look gritty and hard, if there is too much grain, it can become very distracting. If you do choose to use high grain in your images, you need to have a good aesthetic reason to do so, and you also have to make sure you know when you've hit the point of too much grain. Basically, if the grain is getting to the point of obscuring the details of your photograph, then you've got too much.

If you ever don't know where to start, I'd say 400 is a good, safe place. It's fast enough to get detail in deep shadows but also will work well with a relatively bright, sunny day. If you still find that your film is coming out overexposed, you can try one or two things. Rather than switching the speed of your film, keep the same film, but tell your camera that the ISO is actually lower than it is. (Set it on 300 or 200). This will allow less light through the sensor. You can also under develop your film to decrease contrast (or slightly over develop for more contrast).

Grain is slightly different when it comes to digital. For one, it's more commonly referred to as noise, and rather than being made up of silver particles, it's made up of pixels. However, the concept works the same way. The more pixels per inch, or ppi, the better the resolution. For typical digital print, the ppi is between 240–300 ppi. Whether it's film or digital, you lose resolution when you crop an image. As such, it's always better to get exactly the frame you want in camera. Not only does cropping destroy image resolution, but it can throw off the aspect ratio if not done proportionately. This can result in funky shaped images.

You can always lower resolution or size if you need to, but you should always save a base copy of an image that is a high resolution and size. If you don't save a base copy and you lower your resolution to 72 ppi (which is standard for internet usage), you will never be able to print that image. Ideally, you'll want to hang on to your original RAW file, and if it's a film scan, make sure it's a TIF. These are best to print from as they hold the most information in the file. JPEGs are commonly used on websites and for submission to competitions, so I would suggest having a copy of each. If you ever need to make changes, you have your RAW to work from, or at least a TIF.

Make sure your images are always good quality from the ISO on. Experiment with ISO and exposure combinations to find the aesthetic that works best for your project.

Tip 3: Mastering Exposure

Exposure is, in my opinion, the most important technical aspect of photography, and you need to master it before you can move on to making good compositions or photographs that really speak to your audience. Exposure literally *is* your picture. Its definition is how much light you allow to affect your photographic surface, and the amount of time you allow it. The elements of your camera that allow you to control your exposure are ISO, shutter speed, and aperture. Each plays a different role in how your exposure turns out. ISO, as we have already discussed, controls the speed at which your camera is sensitive to light. Shutter speed controls how long you allow light in for, and aperture controls how much light is actually coming into the camera.

Let's start out with aperture. If you've always been confused about which way to go with all those numbers on your camera in any given situation, don't worry. You aren't alone, and it's probably largely due to the fact that you don't understand how aperture works. First off, aperture is done in fractions, (even though the numbers aren't written as fractions on your camera). That's why, as the number gets smaller, the aperture gets wider. After all, ½ is much larger than 1/16. Thus, f/2 is much larger than f/16 and lets in a lot more light.

Now, you might be thinking, "There are so many numbers on my camera, how am I ever going to memorize them all? In the past probably fifteen years, camera companies have started also including half stops on cameras. While this may be helpful to some people, I find that it's just another source of confusion for new photographers as they attempt to get to know their cameras. The best thing you can do for yourself is to memorize the standard f/stops, which are typically as follows, though the scale can go up or down a stop or two further sometimes:

- f/2
- f/2.8
- f/4
- f/5.6
- f/8
- f/11
- f/16
- f/22
- f/32
- f/64

The further up the numbers go, the smaller the aperture, and thus, the deeper the depth of field. The smaller the number, the shallower the depth of field and the more light you're letting in. You might be wondering, what is depth of field? Essentially, it's how far into the picture you can see. If what's in focus is mainly in the foreground of an image and the background is all a blur, then you have a shallow depth of field, whereas deep depth of field can allow you to see for miles. Shallow depth of field is mainly used in macro shots, where you want to have less width to your picture and focus in on a specific detail. Shallow depth of field can also be used in conjunction with a long shutter speed in order to create a surrealist, dreamlike effect. Don't confuse a shallow depth of field with allowing everything to be out of focus, however. In order for a photograph to be good and purposeful, you need to have at least one thing in focus for your audience to concentrate on. After all, depth of field is defined as the amount of space between one point in a photo that is in focus and the next.

If you do want every single thing in your photo to be sharp, then you should consider using a deep depth of field. Of course, depending on the conditions you're working in, this may require you to have a very long shutter speed, especially if you go all the way up to the infamous f/64. Deep depths of field are typically used in journalistic work and in landscapes, because the point of a landscape is to see as far and wide as you can.

A little side note on f/64: it's also the name of a very famous group of photographers, who believed (and I'm paraphrasing) that a photograph should differentiate itself from other arts such as painting in order to be recognized as an art in its own right. They thought that photography was a completely different animal, and wanted every picture taken to ring true to life and be as objective as possible. Of course, this then calls into question how something can be objective when made specifically through an individual's eyes. But essentially, they wanted their pictures to capture life and reality. As such, they wanted everything to be super sharp and defined, and were famous for shooting on f/64 almost exclusively.

Next up is shutter speed, and this function determines how long you allow the amount of light you've chosen into your lens. Shutter speed also works on the basis of fractions, but unlike f/stops, that's generally more easily understood. Standard shutter speeds are:

- 30 seconds

- 15 seconds

- 8 seconds

- 4 seconds

- 2 seconds
- 1 second
- ½ second
- ¼
- 1/8
- 1/15
- 1/30
- 1/60
- 1/125
- 1/250
- 1/500
- 1/1000
- 1/2000
- 1/4000

You should remember, even if you just know the basics, that each change in f/stop and each change in shutter speed is exactly one stop of light difference. So, if you adjust your shutter speed to go faster, that means you're letting in a stop less light than you were before, so you have to open up your aperture one stop to compensate. These are called equivalent exposures. There are also some more advanced methods of mastering exposure that I'll be covering in my next tip.

Tip 4: Bracketing, Metering, and Ansel Adams' Zone System

Bracketing

Bracketing is a method used to ensure that you get the proper exposure on any image that you take. To start off, you'll want to meter, and if you don't have or can't afford a meter, (because they can be really expensive) then I find the easiest way to meter is to use either aperture or shutter priority, which is a function present on both analog and digital cameras. Once you decide one input based on what you want, the camera decides the other, giving you a proper exposure . . . usually. But sometimes, maybe you focused the camera on something really dark or really light, which can result in over or underexposure. What do you do in this case? You'd want to use bracketing. So don't delete the initial image, even if it is a little bit off. Just adjust your camera in the direction you think it needs to go, by one stop. Shoot that photo and do it again, if you feel the need. You may also want to adjust in the other direction as well. This way, you have more to choose from later, because things can look a lot different on a computer screen than they do on the small back of your camera. If you're shooting analog, bracketing provides a safety net for you to choose from in case you estimated your exposure wrong.

Bracketing is also a really great technique for when you're shooting a scene that has more than one prevalent lighting condition, such as an area of extreme shadow *and* an area of extreme highlight. If the difference is really extreme, it can be hard for your camera to find a median exposure that works well for both. Ultimately, one area is going to come out incorrectly exposed. To fix this, what you can do is meter for one condition, shoot it properly, then meter for the other and shoot it properly. Then, in post, you combine the two images to have one overall properly exposed scene. In order to get them to line up as closely as possible, you'll want to make use of a tripod so things don't move around.

An extreme version of this technique is commonly referred to as HDR, or High Dynamic Range Imaging, where you try to capture as much of the range of light as possible. Then you take the images and combine them all for an image that can at times look very surreal. In this case, you might want to go as many as four or five stops in either direction to get as much range as possible. Then, Photoshop's HDR capability will combine them all and you can tweak them from there.

Metering

Digital cameras have quite a few metering modes to choose from, and in this section, I'm going to break down the ones that are available with Canon cameras, because that is what I typically shoot when working digitally. The modes are pretty much the same on a Nikon, although they may have different names.

- Spot metering: This is the most focused mode, and I tend to use it a lot because of my skills learned via the zone system. This mode focuses you in on a very small portion of the image, which is represented by a dot on your viewfinder. If you're using zone system principles, then you would use this mode to focus in on your middle grey.

- Partial metering: Like spot metering, this mode focuses on a small area of the frame, however, it's about double the area used in spot metering. The camera then averages the light it finds in this area to give you your exposure. I also find that this can be helpful for metering middle grey, if you have a larger area of it.

- Center weighted average: This is not a mode I would really suggest using, since it takes the whole of the picture into account, completely disregarding focus. It's weighted heavily towards the center, no matter where your focus is. I also find that averaging an exposure doesn't really work out well unless the light (and colors of objects) is fairly even across the entirety of the field.

- Evaluative: Averages the entire frame, like center weighted, but is more strongly weighted toward the focus point.

Overall, I find that I like to use spot and partial metering the most, because you have the most control over where your focus is. Also, you have to remember that exposure doesn't necessarily work like focus. With focus, you want the area that's sharp to be your main point of attention. However, with exposure, you don't always want to meter for your main subject. Instead, you want to meter for middle grey, which is going to give you proper exposure for your midtones, highlights, and shadows. If you meter for an area that's too dark, you'll get an overexposed picture because your camera gets confused and overcompensates. The opposite is true for an underexposed picture. Subject really has nothing to do with it here; it's all about the play of light and dark.

The principle of middle grey comes from the use of Ansel Adams' Zone System, where he divided all the colors you could ever possibly have into ten zones. Zone five is that perfect middle grey, with the lower zones being darker, and the higher zones getting lighter. Each zone is one stop difference than the last. If you make use of a grey card while metering, you'll have a pretty decent chance of getting the correct exposure.

Tip 5: Shooting Modes

Besides full auto, there are four shooting modes to choose from on most standard DSLR cameras. They are: Program mode, or P, Aperture Priority, or A, Shutter Priority, or T, and full manual. Each has its own benefits, and reasons or situations in which they might come in handy. If you've never taken advantage of any of these modes before, or been quite sure what they do, here's your guide.

Program mode

Program mode is something I would describe as kind of like half auto. The camera still figures out the auto exposure for a particular scene, and gives you the combination of shutter speed and aperture it feels is most appropriate. What you can do with program mode, then, is choose a different combination of shutter speed and aperture that is still going to give you an identical exposure. That way, you get the exposure you need, and can also still get the shutter speed or aperture you would prefer without having to do a bunch of complicated math. I feel like this feature is also great when it comes to learning equivalent exposures, since this is exactly what it's for. The situations in which you might need this mode are: if you're a fairly new photographer and you still need some help when it comes to figuring out exposure, if you want to learn equivalent exposures, or if you find depth of field or shutter speed isn't where you want it and you need a quick fix.

Aperture Priority

Aperture priority is exactly what it sounds like . . . it makes aperture the priority. In my mind, it and Shutter Priority are like the step in between program and manual. Aperture Priority and Shutter Priority don't hold your hand quite as much as program does, but they still give you a little bit of help. Since aperture is the priority here, this mode allows you to self-select your aperture. So it's good if you know what style of depth of field you'd like. It will then auto adjust the shutter speed to what it needs to be for that aperture to glean a correct exposure for the conditions.

Shutter Priority

Shutter priority does the exact same thing as aperture priority, except that it makes shutter the most important thing. This is good for things like sports events, where you know that no matter what, you need a fast shutter speed. This could also be good for when you know you want to do a very long exposure. Whether you use aperture or shutter priority more is really up to personal preference. I typically use aperture priority because I care most about shallow depth of field. However, it really is up to personal aesthetic as well as the individual needs of each photograph you make.

Manual Mode

Manual mode gives you full and absolute control over your camera, and that means that you need to have a pretty strong idea of what you're doing. If you're working exclusively on manual, it means you have a good foundation in how aperture, shutter speed, and ISO work. You also know your equivalent exposures and can adjust quickly as needed.

The use of these modes is partially based in experience level, and partially in convenience. There's no saying that even if you are an advanced photographer that you can't use something other than manual. However, you should never, ever use full auto after the first few months of shooting. Use these other modes as learning tools to work your way up to manual, as a way of really getting to know your camera.

Tip 6: Exposure For Film

I feel the need to include a section on exposure for film, short though it may be, because there are photographers who are experimenting with, or at least curious about, the film process. Learning film can be particularly challenging for photographers who have grown up in the digital era and are accustomed to the instant gratification of an image on a monitor and the low expense. I know that I was at first opposed to learning film because I didn't know what it could teach me. Little did I know, it taught me volumes about how to be meticulous with your work, and it taught me how to get a correct exposure nine times out of ten.

Part of the reason that beginners find film so frustrating is due to the fact that black and white film and color film function differently. In essence, color film is less sensitive to light by nature, so if you're a little under or over, you'll be able to bring the information back more easily than you would with black and white that was off. However, that little bit of ease comes at a price that black and white doesn't have: you get to deal with color casts, and with each type of color film, they differ.

Now, in order to know what speed a film is (how sensitive it is to light) you look at the ISO. Lower numbers indicate less sensitive film, meaning you need more light, and higher numbers indicate more sensitive film, which needs less light. However, new film photographers can often be frustrated because their exposure isn't quite what they expected it to be. While this can be due to a misunderstanding of the correct combination of aperture and shutter speed, it can also be due to the ISO of the film being used being slightly more or less than noted on the package. It can vary up to 200 points, and different brands can vary differing amounts. If you're consistently shooting one type of film and you notice that even with correct exposures, it's coming out consistently under or overexposed, try tricking your camera. The way you do this is to set the camera's ISO to the speed you think the film actually is. So if you have an ISO 100 film that is consistently underexposed, try setting it at 300 and seeing if it comes out correctly. This makes the camera think that the film is more sensitive than it is, letting more light into the sensor and making a correct exposure.

Remember that even if you figure out the correct ISO for one type of film, it's not going to be universal for different companies, which will have a different formula for their film. It takes a lot of trial and error, but once you get it down, you should be good to go.

Tip 7: How to Shoot in Different Light Conditions

This book is all about exposure, and obviously, different conditions are going to call for different exposures, or else everyone could be a photographer. This section should give you a better idea of how to photograph in differing conditions, be it indoor or outdoor, low light or daytime. Let's start with the conditions that are optimal for you to shoot in, and then we can move on to situations that are a bit trickier.

Everyone who isn't a photographer always assumes that the best conditions to shoot in are bright sunny days. And while you can make this aesthetic work for you (look at Urban Outfitters with all their sun flare) it isn't optimal for getting consistently good photos during a shoot. Rather, you want a situation where the light is more even across the entire plane. For this, I really love overcast days, because the sun is filtered through the clouds, creating really pleasing, even light. It's also easy for your subjects because the light isn't harsh on their faces, and it's not too hot. Overcast days are regularly used in fashion photography to get even light and good colors, and then bright blue skies are Photoshopped in after the fact.

Now, if you have to shoot at a time of the day which is not ideal, such as high noon, or a particularly bright morning, it's good to find some shade. Things like trees or even building overhangs can be good for diffusing hard, harsh shadows. When you shoot in harsh light, you risk dark, deep shadows that you aren't creating or controlling, and very, very bright light that blows out highlights. Not only would I suggest finding and making use of shade, but I would also suggest bringing reflectors and a bounce umbrella to help further direct the light.

Sundown and dawn are also lovely. They each create a very different kind of light because the sun is coming from a different part of the sky, (I would say, for example, that dawn has a much softer quality than sundown, which is richer and more jewel toned), but the conditions are similar in that they create even, ambient light all around. Also, in neither situation is the sun fully up, so there's less squinting going on. Dawn and sundown are both referred to as the Golden Hour, and they really are ideal. You just have to be willing to get up early, or be prepared to shoot quickly before you lose the light. You typically have about half an hour in either situation where the light stays even and lovely.

So what about other light conditions that are still aesthetically valid, but are much harder to shoot in? Conditions I would classify here would be: backlighting, night time, and indoor photography.

Now, don't get me wrong. Backlighting can be, and is, absolutely lovely when done correctly, but it can be a hard technique to master because it's so easy for the background to become overwhelming and completely blow out the highlights. The trick is that you have to direct your camera to focus, and meter off of, your subject's face, as opposed to metering off of the backlighting. If you meter off the backlighting, then the camera will overcompensate and your image will be underexposed. Sometimes, no matter what you do, the metering can be really difficult, and you might have to take two separate exposures and superimpose them to get one good, solid exposure. Practice is key with this technique.

What about night photography? This is really tricky because a lot of people think that you can just pump up the ISO and you're good to go. While it is true that you do need to make your camera more sensitive to light, you don't want to just set it at 3200 or 6400 and shoot. Your images will more than likely come out super grainy and washed out looking, and that's not a good aesthetic. So what can you do? First off, since there is going to be a lot less light coming into the sensor, do put your ISO higher than normal, but start off at a reasonable 800 or 1200 and work your way up from there. To minimize shake, which is already going to be present, put your camera on a tripod before you start to shoot. Decide whether or not you want to use a mounted flash or whether you want to try a really long exposure. Both are going to give you an extremely different look, so if you are unsure of what you want, I would suggest trying both. With your flash, you might want to use the camera flash in conjunction with the mounted flash as a fill flash to avoid the washed out look the on camera flash typically produces. It'll take some experimenting to get it right, depending on how dark it is, what you're attempting to photograph, and the method you choose to go about it.

Indoor photography has much of the same rules as night photography. You don't necessarily have to worry about a high ISO unless you are working in a low lighting situation, but I would still definitely suggest the use of a tripod and a flash. The tripod is good for indoor situations because it is possible that you'll be dealing with the movement of other people around you as you're trying to shoot, such as at a party or gathering. The use of a flash can be good to offset the surrounding ambient light, especially if that light is of the fluorescent variety. You can also use a bounce and/or reflectors indoors if need be.

Remember that none of the situations mentioned here are ideal studio situations, but rather, my tips for on location shoots. Trying to shoot outside with natural, even light is always my go to and best bet, but make use of these tips even when you aren't in ideal lighting situations. They will help to make the photo more flattering overall.

Tip 8: Editing In Camera RAW

Your RAW file is what I like to think of as a sort of digital negative. If you have Camera RAW and you've just been closing it out to work in main Photoshop, you've been doing it all wrong. Believe me, it took me a while to figure out as well. But the reason you should be editing in RAW is that the file contains more information in the highlights and the darks than any other file format.

This is great because both of these are problem areas for a lot of photographers, new and old. In Camera RAW, you can save an image that would otherwise be unsalvageable. Pull up as much information as you can in RAW and save it as a master, just as you would an initial film scan, before making smaller adjustments in the main Photoshop program.

Tip 9: Editing Film For Exposure

I had been scanning film for years before my professor pointed out to me that I was doing it completely wrong. I learned on Imacons, and I had been working with the Flextight software quite as if it were Photoshop. No wonder I got confused . . . the first professor that had taught me to scan hadn't quite gone in-depth, and a lot of the controls seemed much the same. I was under the impression that you were supposed to make the image look how you wanted your finished product to look. So I was pushing my highlights, losing detail, making them too dark. My other lovely professor corrected me, saying that actually, the end result of a good scan looks really flat and dull. The purpose of a scan is like that of a RAW file . . . to have the best baseline with the most information possible in the file. In order to do this, you want to make sure that you can see every detail, every bit of information in the photograph. That often means tamping down shadows you want to be deep or highlights you want to be bright for the sake of being able to see what's going on there. The end result is often very grey, but remember that this is just a starting point; you're going to take the finished scan into Photoshop later and make it look aesthetically how you want it to. Make sure that you make those changes on a copy of the image so that you have a master copy if you ever decide to completely alter your aesthetic.

You also want to make sure that you're scanning at the highest possible ppi that your scanner and computer can handle. This will help give you the clearest, most crisp information possible. As always, you'll want to save a 300 ppi copy to print from, and a 72 ppi version for web, but make sure your master copy is very large.

No matter what kind of scanner you have, these are two rules you want to follow. If, like me, you now only have access to a flatbed scanner, also make sure that you set it on professional mode to get the highest quality image possible.

Conclusion

Hopefully, with the conclusion of this short book, you have a better idea of what exposure is and what it means to the overall quality of your photo. You know that exposure is the very thing that creates the image. You know that a triad of aperture, shutter speed, and ISO creates that exposure. You understand grain and you know how to capture a generally solid exposure in camera to begin with.

If you make a minor mistake, you know how to fix it in RAW or on a scanner. The most important thing, technically, about a photograph, is to get the most information out of it as you can.

In the case of film, it's better to overexpose than to underexpose, because overexposure means that at least the information got captured on the film and it's present to be burned in. However, with digital the opposite is true because it's much easier to lift information out of the shadows than it is to bring it back in if it's blown out.

If you pay attention to the craft of your photos from start to finish, you will get the most information possible, resulting in a rich, high quality image.

www.ingramcontent.com/pod-product-compliance
Lightning Source LLC
Chambersburg PA
CBHW070754180526
45168CB00004B/1604